J
973.931
Marco
Marcovitz, Hal

Guardians of Safety

D1171487

United We Stand
AMERICA RESPONDS TO THE EVENTS OF
September 11, 2001

CALL TO RESCUE, CALL TO HEAL
Emergency Medical Professionals at Ground Zero

FIRST TO ARRIVE
Firefighters at Ground Zero

GUARDIANS OF SAFETY
Law Enforcement at Ground Zero

HELPING HANDS
A City and a Nation Lend Their Support at Ground Zero

KEEPING THE PEACE
The U.S. Military Responds to Terror

WE THE PEOPLE
The U.S. Government's United Response Against Terror

United We Stand
AMERICA RESPONDS TO THE EVENTS OF
September 11, 2001

GUARDIANS OF SAFETY

Law Enforcement at Ground Zero

Hal Marcovitz

CHELSEA HOUSE
PUBLISHERS
A Haights Cross Communications Company

PHILADELPHIA

FRONTIS: Officers in Pasadena, California wearing "NYPD" bands across their badges pay tribute to the New York Police Department during a ceremony held on December 11, 2001. Police officers across the country shared the grief of their fallen comrades in New York City.

CHELSEA HOUSE PUBLISHERS

EDITOR IN CHIEF Sally Cheney
DIRECTOR OF PRODUCTION Kim Shinners
CREATIVE MANAGER Takeshi Takahashi
MANUFACTURING MANAGER Diann Grasse

STAFF FOR GUARDIANS OF SAFETY

ASSOCIATE EDITOR Benjamin Xavier Kim
PICTURE RESEARCHER Sarah Bloom
PRODUCTION ASSISTANT Jaimie Winkler
COVER AND SERIES DESIGNER Keith Trego
LAYOUT 21st Century Publishing and Communications, Inc.

A Haights Cross Communications Company

http://www.chelseahouse.com

First Printing

1 3 5 7 9 8 6 4 2

Library of Congress Cataloging-in-Publication Data

Marcovitz, Hal.
    Guardians of safety: law enforcement at Ground Zero / Hal Marcovitz.
        p. cm.
Includes index.
Summary: Examines the history of law enforcement in New York City, as well as the response of law enforcement agencies to the terrorist attacks on the World Trade Center on September 11, 2001.
    ISBN 0-7910-6960-5
    1. Police—New York (State)—New York—Juvenile literature.
2. Police—New York (State)—New York—History—Juvenile literature.
3. Law enforcement—New York (State)—New York—History—
Juvenile literature. 4. Terrorism—New York (State)—New York—
History—Juvenile literature. 5. September 11 Terrorist Attacks, 2001
—Juvenile literature. [1. Police—New York (State)—New York.
2. Police—New York (State)—New York—History. 3. September 11
Terrorist Attacks, 2001.] I. Title.
HV8148.N52 M27 2002
973.931—dc21
                                                        2002007534

TABLE OF CONTENTS

11/2003
RAINBOW
$20.75

FOREWORD by Benjamin Xavier Kim   6

IN THE LINE OF DUTY   9

NONE ARE SAFE   17

THE BLAZE OF REVOLUTION   27

MODERN-DAY TERROR   37

RETRACING AL-QAEDA   43

THE BATTLE IS JOINED   51

BIBLIOGRAPHY   58

WEBSITES   60

ORGANIZATIONS AND AGENCIES   61

FURTHER READING   62

INDEX   63

Foreword

The events of September 11, 2001 will be remembered as one of the most devastating attacks on American soil ever. The terrorist attacks caused not only physical destruction but also shattered America's sense of safety and security, and highlighted the fact that there were many groups in the world that did not embrace the United States and its far-reaching influence. While things have, for the most part, returned to normal, there is still no escaping the demarcation of life before and after September 11—the newest day that will forever live in infamy.

Yet, even in the aftermath of the terror and destruction, one can see some positive effects that have arisen from the attacks. Americans' interest in foreign countries—especially those where Islam is the predominant religion—and U.S. foreign policy has been at an all-time high. The previously mundane occupations of firefighter, police officer and emergency medical worker have taken on a newfound level of respect due to the heroism and selflessness displayed on September 11. The issue of airport security has finally been taken seriously with the implementation of National Guardsmen in airports and undercover air marshals on board flights.

The books in this series tell the story of how various groups and agencies dealt with the unfolding events of September 11. They also tell the history of these agencies and how they have dealt with other crises in the past, as well as how they are operating in the wake of September 11.

While the rest of us were reeling in shock and horror at what was unfolding before our eyes, there were others whose jobs required that they confront the situation head-on. These are their stories.

Benjamin Xavier Kim
Series Editor

Less than two hours after being struck by two highjacked passenger airplanes, the towers of the World Trade Center collapsed amid an explosive shower of debris. Many police officers and firefighters lost their lives while trying to help trapped office workers leave the burning buildings.

In the Line of Duty

Moira Smith loved adventure. She would drag her husband James to amusement parks where the couple rode terrifying rollercoasters. One summer, the Smiths vacationed in Spain, where Moira insisted on taking part in the annual ritual of running with the bulls through the streets of Pamplona. Each morning during the Festival of San Fermín, runners dash along the ancient cobblestone streets of the city while chased by dangerous bulls. It is not unusual for runners to be injured and, over the years, there have been several deaths. Still, Moira was not put off by the danger, and she delightedly made the run.

Her job contained an element of danger as well. In 1988, she joined the New York Police Department. Soon, she earned a reputation as a dedicated cop willing to put herself in harm's way if she had to. To other cops, she was known as a "buff"—a police officer who loved her job. "It means you do more than other people expect you to," said husband James Smith, also a New York police officer. "It means you're a hero."

Just after 8:45 A.M. on September 11, 2001, dispatchers in the NYPD communications center received a radio call from Officer Moira Smith, who was on duty in Lower Manhattan. The dispatchers almost couldn't believe what Smith told them—that an airliner had apparently just crashed into the north tower of the World Trade Center, one of the world's tallest skyscrapers. Smith told the dispatchers to send police and fire units to the tower. She also told them that she was headed into the tower along with her partner Robert Fazio to help evacuate some of the 50,000 people who worked in the building.

Meanwhile, John O'Neill was in his office on the 34th floor of the north tower when the plane hit. A former agent of the Federal Bureau of Investigation, O'Neill had recently been hired as head of security for the World Trade Center. O'Neill was an expert in anti-terrorism measures at the FBI, and had been lured away from the bureau by the Port Authority of New York and New Jersey, which owns the World Trade Center. Officials at the Port Authority were concerned that the massive building could be the target of terrorists; after all, in 1993 Arab extremists detonated a bomb in the basement of the building, killing six people, injuring 1,000 and causing some $250 million damage to the complex. Although the World Trade Center's two main towers withstood the blast, the Port Authority was deeply worried that the buildings were still a likely target for terrorism, and they hoped that O'Neill could lend his expertise to make the twin towers safe from terrorists. On September 11, he had been in his new job for just 20 days.

That morning, John O'Neill Jr. caught a train to New York City from his home in Wilmington, Delaware. O'Neill was heading to New York that day to visit his father in his new office. As the train approached New York, O'Neill gazed out the window and saw smoke billowing from the World Trade Center. He called his father on a cell phone.

"He said he was OK," John O'Neill Jr. recalled. "He was on his way out to assess the damage."

NYPD Detective Dan Richards was totally devoted to his job. An 18-year member of the NYPD, Richards had never married, so he never felt the responsibility to make it home for dinner on time. What's more, Richards joined the NYPD's bomb squad—the elite force of officers who take on the dangerous assignment of defusing explosives. In 1996, Richards took a leave of absence from the NYPD and volunteered to be part of the United Nations international police force that served in the war-torn nation of Bosnia-Herzegovina, where he helped disarm land mines and other bombs.

"Dan Richards was the kind of man who knew the difference between right and wrong, and he knew the difference between difficult and easy, but he would never let something difficult stand between him and doing something right," said his friend, Detective Dan McNally. "He was a man who was comfortable in his own skin."

Dan Richards was on duty September 11. When the plane hit, he rushed to the World Trade Center that morning as well.

Unknown to Moira Smith, John O'Neill, Dan Richards, and the hundreds of other law enforcement officers called to duty that morning, the World Trade Center had just been struck by an airliner that was hijacked by terrorists. While hundreds of police officers and New York firemen worked feverishly to evacuate people from the north tower, a second hijacked airliner smashed into the south tower. Elsewhere, a third jet crashed into the Pentagon in Washington, while in rural western Pennsylvania near Pittsburgh, a fourth jet plummeted to the ground in a wooded area. It is believed that airliner was heading for

John O'Neill had recently accepted a job as head of security at the World Trade Center when the terrorist attacks tragically ended his life. The former FBI agent had just entered the South Tower when it suddenly collapsed. Here, his flag-draped casket is carried from St. Nicholas Church in Atlantic City, NJ, following funeral services.

a target in Washington—possibly the White House—when passengers bravely overpowered the terrorists and sacrificed their lives to force it down before it could cause major devastation.

There is no question, though, that the terrorists achieved their goal when the planes struck the World Trade Center. Within an hour of the collisions, the giant towers gave way to the intense fire that erupted when the jet fuel aboard the planes exploded. Both towers collapsed, sending millions of tons of concrete, steel and glass crashing to the street below.

Incredibly, of the estimated 50,000 people inside the towers, some 47,000 made it out safely. Many of them owed their lives to the police officers and firefighters who responded to the emergency, bravely entering the World Trade Center to help with the evacuation.

Many of those police officers and firefighters died when the towers collapsed. Moira Smith, James O'Neill, and Dan Richards were among the members of the law enforcement community who sacrificed their lives in the line of duty that day. The grim total included 23 officers from the New York Police Department and 37 members of the Port Authority police. For the New York Fire Department, the loss was even more devastating. Some 350 firefighters lost their lives that day.

When Dan Richards and Dan McNally arrived at the World Trade Center, both towers were on fire and thousands of workers and visitors were already streaming out of the buildings.

Port Authority policeman, Sergeant John McLoughlin, was helping to evacuate the south tower when the building collapsed. Luckily, he found a tiny crawl space that withstood the crash, where he remained—with two broken legs—until seismic equipment located sounds he made inside the rubble. Rescue workers then dug him out from beneath some 40 feet of debris.

"All I thought about was my family. I had to get out for them. I'm not saying there weren't points of sheer desperation. There was a point of acceptance of dying. Once they started digging, I knew I was getting out."

Sergeant John McLoughlin

The World Trade Center is actually a complex of seven build-ings. Clearly, if the two twin towers were in danger of toppling over, workers in the other buildings were in danger as well. McNally and Richards headed for Building 6 in the complex to help with the evacuation there.

The north tower collapsed just before 10 A.M. Richards and McNally were outside Building 6 when tons of debris started raining down on them. Both men scrambled for cover. McNally survived the collapse, but Richards was buried under tons of debris. His body was never found.

"It would sound very cliché to say he died as he lived, helping people," said McNally. "The guy was a New York City detective who was on the bomb squad for 15 years. He had placed his life in harm's way many, many times. This is just another time that tempted fate."

After speaking with his son by cell phone, John O'Neill made it outside where, amid the chaos around him, he spotted a familiar face: Wesley Wong, an FBI agent who had raced over to the building when he heard news reports of the collisions.

"He asked me if there was any information I could divulge," Wong said. "One of the questions he asked me was, 'Is it true the Pentagon had been hit?'"

At that point, O'Neill drifted away. Wong said he last saw O'Neill heading into the south tower. O'Neill's body was recovered in the rubble by rescue workers on September 21.

A news photographer captured an image of Moira Smith leading an injured man out of the north tower. Over her police radio, Smith kept in constant communication with dispatch-ers, giving them details of where she was and what she was doing. Just before 10:30 A.M., Smith reported that she was on the third floor of the south tower, helping an asthma sufferer escape. "Don't look, keep moving," Smith told people as she helped herd them to safety.

And then, the south tower collapsed on top of her and

New York Mayor Rudolph Giuliani was quick to recognize the sacrifices made by police and fire personnel on September 11th. In a ceremony held October 4, 2001, he presented Medals of Honor to the family members of those who gave their lives that fateful day.

others. Moira Smith's body was finally recovered on March 20, 2002.

"We've undergone some tremendous losses, and we're going to grieve for them horribly," said New York Mayor Rudolph Giuliani.

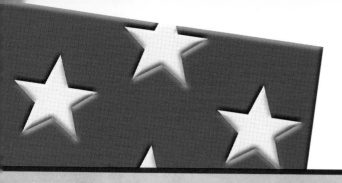

In the early 19th century, New York was a rapidly growing city where people of many different cultures lived and worked. As crowding and crime increased, it became clear that the city's outdated system of marshals, constables, and night watchmen was unable to enforce the law effectively. In 1845, after pressure from newspapers like the *New York Herald*, the city created a centralized police department.

2

None Are Safe

B y the 1830s, New York had grown into a bustling city of nearly 300,000 people. The city's harbor was an important commercial shipping port, which helped New York become America's premier center of trade. Additionally, poor and oppressed immigrants from Europe's ailing monarchies were just starting to make their way to America; in the coming decades, the trickle that was just beginning in the 1830s would explode into a deluge. Millions of those immigrants would enter America through New York Harbor, and many of them chose to make their homes in the city.

As New York grew, so did its problems. One of those problems was street crime. Murders, assaults and robberies became common occurrences on New York streets. The city's authorities soon found themselves ill-equipped to deal with the growth of crime. Since colonial days, the enforcement of laws in New York had been the responsibility of a smorgasbord of peace officers, including a small force of elected constables, marshals appointed by the mayor and, finally, members of the "night watch"—citizens who worked part-time at night to keep order on city streets, but had powers to arrest criminals only when they actually saw them commit a crime. Few of the night watchmen or constables were trained in the techniques of law enforcement, even as they existed in the 1830s. Indeed, the night watchmen were known mostly for sleeping on duty. The marshals, who were supposed to be professional police officers charged with investigating crimes and tracking down thugs and bunco artists, were usually inept cronies who owed their jobs to political insiders and others with influence in City Hall.

Meanwhile, a phenomena was occurring on street corners in the city that had captured the attention of New Yorkers. On September 3, 1833, the *New York Sun* commenced publication. The *Sun* was the first of the "penny press" daily newspapers that sold for just a penny, hawked on street corners by boys who would shout out the headlines to New Yorkers as they hurried along to work. Soon, other penny press papers would compete with the *Sun*.

One of those papers was the *New York Herald*, which commenced publication in 1835. The *Herald* was owned by James Gordon Bennett, an immigrant from Scotland who quickly concluded that penny press readers were hooked on news about the gritty life of New York's streets—which included crime news. Bennett was one of the first publishers to dispatch his paper's reporters to the city's criminal courts, where they found news of arrests, convictions, and—as Bennett soon learned—police ineptitude.

For Bennett, the opportunity to point out the shortcomings of the police arrived in 1836 when a prostitute named Helen Jewett was found brutally murdered in a city brothel. Suspicion soon fell on 19-year-old Richard Robinson, a wealthy playboy and regular customer of Jewett's brothel. Robinson was arrested and charged with Jewett's murder.

Bennett, however, was convinced that Robinson was innocent, and he aimed to use the resources of the *Herald* to harp on the incompetence of the investigators who worked on the case. As the case neared trial, the *Herald* reported that Robinson was a "young, amiable and innocent youth" framed by the "the police establishment, which is rotten to the heart." Bennett even went so far as to name his own suspect: Rosina Townsend, the madam in the brothel where Jewett worked. Townsend, Bennett's readers learned, had "the eyes of the devil."

Finally, the case came to trial. Robinson's lawyers contended that the witnesses —most of whom were prostitutes or the customers of prostitutes—were unreliable and had been goaded into testifying against their client by the corrupt marshals and constables of New York. The

In 1835, Scottish immigrant James Gordon Bennett founded the *New York Herald*—among the first "penny press" daily newspapers in New Yorkers. Bennett criticized the city's inept law enforcement system and called for the creation of a modern police force. Ten years later, his dream became a reality.

jury bought the story, and after deliberating just three hours acquitted Robinson of the murder.

The Jewett case made it clear that New York's law enforcement system was corrupt and incapable of dealing with big city crime. No one realized that more than James Gordon Bennett, who started using his newspaper to call for establishment of a professionally trained full-time police department. By 1842, Bennett had successfully goaded New York City Council into establishing a committee to examine the state of law enforcement in the city. It surprised no one when the committee concluded that the constables, marshals, and night watchmen were not meeting the needs of New Yorkers.

"Dwellings and warehouses are entered with ease and apparent coolness and carelessness of detection which show that none are safe. Thronged as our city is, men are robbed in the street. Thousands that are arrested go unpunished and the defenseless and the beautiful are ravished and murdered in the day time, and no trace of criminal is found. The man of business, in his lawful calling at the most public corner of our city, is slaughtered in the sunshine and packed up and sent away by the most public and known channels of trade, and suspicion is hardly excited," the committee wrote in its final report.

In 1844, the New York State Legislature passed a law authorizing creation of a professional New York City police force of 800 officers. On May 23, 1845, the city council accepted an ordinance adopting the 1844 law, and the New York Police Department was born.

Meanwhile, events unfolding across the Atlantic Ocean would soon have an impact on New York's new police department. In Ireland, the potato crop failed, and the resulting famine caused 2.5 million Irish citizens to flee the poverty of their homeland. More than 1 million of them immigrated to America and most settled in New York. By the 1850s, the NYPD was taking on a decidedly Irish flavor. So many Irish immigrants had arrived by then and had become naturalized citizens that the city's political leaders realized they represented a substantial voting bloc. So to curry favor in the Irish community, politicians promised city jobs to Irish-born New Yorkers. Many of those people found their way onto the police force.

The NYPD faced its first real test in July 1863. With the Civil War raging in the South, the federal government found it necessary to institute the nation's first military draft. What was particularly riling to most able-bodied men was a provision of the draft law that enabled draftees to buy their way out of the Union Army for $300—an incredible amount of money in those days and, certainly, a sum none but the rich could afford.

New York's political leaders were Democrats, and they rarely let an opportunity pass to criticize Republican President Abraham Lincoln. They spent weeks crisscrossing the city, speaking out against Lincoln and the unfairness of the draft law. By July, tempers had reached feverish levels. When Army Captain Joel Erhardt traipsed into New York City neighborhoods to begin taking names of construction workers for the draft, he was chased off by angry protesters wielding lead pipes.

On July 13, during one of the first drawings of names for the draft, a mob gathered outside the city draft office. The drawing started just after 10 A.M. Soon, members of the mob started shouting complaints toward the officials conducting the draft. Quickly, the mob became bolder and started surging toward the draft office. After 20 minutes, the draft was suspended. Officials quickly abandoned the office. Sixty police officers had been dispatched to control the mob, but they were soon overmatched. The mob attacked the draft office and burned it down.

Draft riots soon erupted across the city. Rioters set fires, heaved bricks and rocks through store windows, tore down telegraph poles and cut wires. They targeted munitions factories that were providing arms for the Union Army as well as pro-war newspapers, including Horace Greeley's *New York Tribune*. Looters ran rampant through the destruction.

At first, the mobs gained the upper hand over the police, who didn't seem to know how to deal with the rioters. Several officers were caught alone and savagely beaten by rioters. Free blacks also found themselves targeted by the mobs. Black neighborhoods in the city had to be evacuated when the mobs attacked. Some blacks were lynched by the rioters.

As the week wore on, the police slowly gained the advantage.

The first real test for the NYPD came with the draft riots of the
Civil War. Designed to increase Union manpower, the country's
first use of a military draft allowed wealthy citizens to buy their
way out of army service for a fee of $300. Spurred by Democrats,
working-class New Yorkers protested, and a series of brutal riots
broke out throughout the city. With the help of the army, the
NYPD was able to restore peace.

Aided by Union Army troops summoned to New York City from
the war front, the police and troops showed a relentless brutality
when they encountered mobs of rioting citizens. The police reacted
by swinging their heavy nightsticks or simply firing volleys
into the crowds.

By July 18 the mobs had been broken and order was returned
to the city. In New York, the Union's cause started gaining more
popularity as well. During the summer of 1863 the tide turned
in the Union's favor. When Generals Ulysses S. Grant and
William Tecumseh Sherman started winning important victories
over the rebel armies, New Yorkers found themselves sharing in
the national euphoria.

The New York police emerged from the draft riots as heroes, but they didn't stay heroes for long. By the 1890s, the NYPD as well as most other agencies of the city government were bloated with political appointees who owed their jobs to New York's corrupt Tammany Hall political machine, which had dominated the New York Democratic Party for decades. In the state capital of Albany, a committee headed by Republican State Senator Clarence Lexow started investigating corruption in the city government.

It didn't take the Lexow Committee long to find corruption in the New York City police. Police officers were found to be taking bribes from gamblers, madams and illegal saloonkeepers who paid the cops to avoid arrest. Tammany politicians were charged with paying police officers to help them fix elections. Some police officers were charged with paying politicians to find them jobs or promotions at the NYPD.

At the time, the NYPD was headed by an official with the rank of superintendent. In 1886, Superintendent William Murray admitted that although his salary was never more than $3,500 a year, his personal worth could be valued at some $300,000—an incredible fortune for the era, which in today's dollars would qualify the superintendent as a millionaire many times over. He was replaced by Superintendent Thomas Byrnes, who found himself called before the Lexow Committee. Like Murray, Byrnes was forced to admit that although he had worked his entire adult life on the NYPD, he was now a wealthy man due to bribery. Clearly, it was time for a reformer.

Theodore Roosevelt was a wealthy New Yorker, born to privilege and raised in the city's fashionable East Side. He spent his summers at his family's country home in Long Island or taking long tours of Europe and Asia. Despite his upbringing, Roosevelt was by no means a rich snob. He enjoyed rough-and-tumble sports such as boxing and wrestling and had, in fact, spent years in sweaty New York City gyms refining his skills against some of the city's best prizefighters. Just 36 years old in 1895, Roosevelt had started carving himself out a career as a writer and member of the New York State Legislature representing a wealthy Manhattan district in

Albany when he resigned to take a job in Washington as a member of the U.S. Civil Service Commission. Roosevelt soon grew bored with the life of a federal bureaucrat. When political friends approached him about taking over the New York Police Department and ridding it of corruption, Roosevelt jumped at the chance. On May 6, 1895, Theodore Roosevelt walked into NYPD headquarters at 300 Mulberry Street, having been named to the newly appointed post of police commissioner.

Roosevelt's first job was to get rid of the corruption at the top of the department. Byrnes was one of the first to go; the superintendent submitted his retirement papers just 21 days after Roosevelt took over. Meanwhile, Roosevelt made unannounced visits to the city precinct houses, often dropping in on unsuspecting officers at 4 A.M. and flying into a rage if he found them sleeping at their desks. Roosevelt often invited newspaper reporters along on the surprise visits, knowing their stories would embarrass the lazy cops.

"There had been in previous years the most widespread and gross corruption in connection with every activity in the Police Department, and there had been a regular tariff for appointments and promotions," Roosevelt wrote. "Many powerful politicians and many corrupt outsiders believed that in some way or other it would still be possible to secure appointments by corrupt and improper methods, and many good citizens felt the same conviction. I endeavored to remove the impression from the minds of both sets of people by giving the widest publicity to what we were doing and how we were doing it, by making the whole process open and aboveboard, and by making it evident that we would probe to the bottom every charge of corruption."

Roosevelt took other steps to improve the department. He set up training programs for officers and recruited patrolmen from outside the city, which he hoped would lure officers with more education to the ranks. During his two years as police commissioner, he oversaw the hiring of some 1,700 new cops. He also standardized the department's weapons, issuing each officer a

THE CEREMONY OF SUBMISSION.

By the late 1800s, New York's corrupt political bosses drew the attention of state investigators. The bribery and election-fixing activities exposed by the Tammany Hall scandal revealed corruption at nearly all levels of law enforcement. As this cartoon shows, Tammany Hall's Boss Tweed (seen here as an enthroned tiger) had forced the city into submission. Tweed and other corrupt bosses were eventually tried, convicted, and jailed.

.32-caliber revolver and made sure training courses in proper use of firearms were provided.

Roosevelt left the police department in 1897. With trouble brewing in Cuba, Roosevelt was anxious to become part of the national government again. He won an appointment as assistant secretary of the Navy, then resigned at the outbreak of the Spanish-American War, joining a swashbuckling cavalry unit known as the Rough Riders. After the war, he rode his celebrity status into the White House.

As New York City entered the 20th century, new threats to peaceful living arose. Spurred by the communist revolution in Russia, anarchists like Alexander Berkman (seen here at a 1914 rally) called for the violent over-throw of the government. Bombings and other attacks became a more common feature of daily life.

3

The Blaze of Revolution

While Theodore Roosevelt was busy reforming the New York police, the officers under his control as well as law enforcement agencies elsewhere had their wary eyes on a growing movement in America they found to be particularly troubling. Immigrants from Europe were joining the anarchist movement in America, advocating a violent overthrow of the federal government in favor of a socialist regime. As far back as the 1870s, New York city detectives had been watching Schwab's Saloon, where German immigrant Johann Most was known to frequent. In Europe, Most advocated anarchism, but had worn out his welcome there. So he brought his message to America, where the U.S. Constitution guaranteed him free speech. In New York, Most published a radical newspaper that often advocated the assassination of government leaders.

One of his devoted readers was Leon Czolgosz. In 1901, Czolgosz assassinated President William McKinley in Buffalo, New York. It would be the beginning of a radical era in America that would see the rise of such anarchist leaders as Emma Goldman and Alexander Berkman, both of whom would be deported for the advocacy of violence. In 1917, the Bolsheviks overthrew Czar Nicholas II in Russia and established a communist regime. Many anarchists believed a similar revolution could succeed in America.

On June 2, 1919, anarchists exploded a bomb on the doorstep of U.S. Attorney General A. Mitchell Palmer in Washington. The bomb tore away much of the front of the attorney general's house, killing the hapless anarchist who set the explosive. Palmer and his family were not injured by the blast.

Palmer's house wasn't the only target. Eight other bombs were set around Washington that night while another 38 were detonated at the offices and homes of government officials in other cities. Many buildings were damaged in the explosions but, miraculously, no one was hurt.

Palmer acted quickly. He ordered the Justice Department's Bureau of Investigation—the forerunner of the FBI— to swoop down on the anarchists. Thus began the era of the so-called Palmer Raids, in which federal agents rounded up hundreds of suspected "Reds"—as well as many innocent people—and deported them back to their European homelands.

"Like a prairie fire, the blaze of revolution was sweep-ing over every American institution of law and order. . . . It was eating its way into the homes of the American work-men, its sharp tongues of revolutionary heat were licking the altars of the churches, leaping into the belfry of the school bell, crawling into the sacred corners of American homes, seeking to replace marriage vows with libertine laws, burning up the foundations of society," Palmer wrote in defense of his raids.

The anarchists retaliated. On September 16, 1920, an anarchist drove a horse-drawn wagon onto Wall Street in the heart of the New York financial district. Quietly, the anarchist stepped off the wagon and walked away. Minutes later, just before noon, the wagon exploded. Obviously, it was the anarchist's intention to detonate the bomb as the noon lunch crowd flooded out of the office buildings that lined Wall Street. The explosion killed 38 innocent people and injured hundreds of others. The NYPD raced to the scene but found it could do little for the victims. The explosion caused extensive damage along Wall Street —even shutting down the New York Stock Exchange for the day.

From the start, the NYPD suspected anarchists were to blame. An investigation commenced immediately.

The day after the blast, the *New York Times* reported that "All phases of the various investigations lasted far into the night and will be resumed early this morning. It was said last

POLICE DOGS

Dogs have been a part of police work since the late 1800s in Ghent, Belgium. The success of the Ghent police dogs caught the attention of law enforcement officials in Europe, and by 1910, police departments in Germany, Austria, Hungary and Italy followed suit. In 1907, New York became the first American city to establish its own "K-9" unit. By 1970, more than 80 American police departments had established K-9 units.

At Ground Zero, the dogs proved particularly effective for search and rescue. Pup-Dog, a Labrador from Boulder, Colorado, was credited with finding eight bodies in the 11 days he spent at Ground Zero.

On September 16, 1920 an anarchist detonated a wagonload of explosives in front of the New York Stock Exchange, killing 38 people and wounding many others. Despite a thorough investigation by the NYPD, the crime was never solved.

night that (police) were investigating the recent movements of every person in the city of known radical tendencies and that, unless definite evidence should lead elsewhere, they would continue this phase of their work until every person who might be expected to have any possible knowledge of the affair had been examined."

In the days that followed the blast, few clues were found in the rubble. Detectives from the NYPD tracked down hundreds of leads, even visiting each of the city's 4,000 stables in the hopes that the horseshoes from the owner of the dead animal that pulled the wagon could be identified. But the search proved fruitless. To this day, the NYPD has never solved the Wall Street bombing of 1920.

As the word suggests, *terrorists* attempt to terrorize, or strike fear, into a society or group of people by threatening or committing acts of violence. Indeed, they desire their acts to be public displays of violence so their message is heard and understood by as many people as possible. In the end, they hope to achieve political goals, such as changing conditions in society or even overthrowing a government.

Terrorists are frequently members of groups, although they usually act alone or in small squads known as "cells." The identities of their leaders and members are often kept secret, making it difficult for law enforcement agencies to track them down or defeat the larger group: while the individual terrorist or terrorist cell may be captured or killed, the organization remains intact and authorities can only guess at its precise structure and membership.

Terrorists may target governments, political parties, ethnic or religious groups, corporations or members of the news media. Sometimes they carry out political assassinations, but most often the violence is directed at random victims— passengers on a bus or airplane, for example, or young people dancing in a nightclub or shopping at a mall. The randomness of the attack serves an important terrorist goal: bringing fear to, and undermining the sense of security of, large numbers of people who realize that they too could be victims simply by being in the wrong place at the wrong time. Many terrorists are willing to give their own lives for the cause, acting as suicide bombers with the belief that their deeds will bring about change. Terrorism is more about sending a message than making victims suffer. That is why terrorist groups are quick to claim responsibility for their crimes and welcome press interest in their activities.

In many areas of the world, terrorism seems to be a way of life. In the Middle East, hijackings and hostage-taking have been some of the more visible acts. Over the years, Americans have also been affected by terrorism. Prior to the attack on the World Trade Center, the worst case of terrorism committed on American soil was the destruction of the Alfred P. Murrah Federal Building in Oklahoma City, Oklahoma, in 1995. The building was destroyed by a bomb that had been set off in a truck parked in front of the building by Timothy McVeigh, who aimed to take revenge on the government for what he believed was the curtailment of people's rights. A total of 168 people died in the blast, including many children in the building's day-care center. McVeigh was charged with the murders; he was convicted and executed in June 2001.

Prior to the Murrah bombing, Americans suffered at the hands of terrorists during an incident on January 24, 1975, in New York City. Just before 1:30 P.M. a bomb exploded in Fraunces Tavern in New York, killing four people and injuring 60. The tavern, which was built in 1719, is one of New York's most historic landmarks. The colonnaded yellow-brick tavern is where George Washington announced his resignation as head of the Continental Army on December 4, 1783.

The tavern is located in the city's financial district, and had remained a popular place for businessmen to enjoy lunch. Indeed, the tavern was packed with diners when the bomb went off, shattering dozens of windows, splintering doors, crumbling walls and collapsing stairways. The explosion was so powerful that it shattered windows in the New York Telephone Company across the street.

An hour after the blast, news organizations received calls from an organization that called itself the Fuerzas Armadas

The 1995 bombing of the Murrah Federal Building in Oklahoma City awakened America to the threat of terrorism from our own citizens. Former soldier Timothy McVeigh was arrested, tried, convicted, and executed for his role in the attack that took 168 lives.

de Liberacion Nacional—the Armed Forces of National Liberation. The group was best known by its acronym, FALN. Its leaders were committed to independence for Puerto Rico. FALN claimed responsibility for the bomb. In a telephone booth not far from the blast site, police found a typewritten note. It read: "We, FALN, the Armed Forces of the Puerto Rican nation, take full responsibility for the especially detonated bomb that exploded today at Fraunces Tavern with reactionary corporate executives inside. The Yanki (American) government is trying to terrorize and kill our people to intimidate us from seeking our rightful independence from colonialism. They do this in the same way as they did in Vietnam, Guatemala, Chile, Argentina, Mexico, the Congo and in many other places, including the United States itself. . . . You have unleashed a storm from which you comfortable Yankis cannot escape. FREE PUERTO RICO RIGHT NOW!"

Since the 1930s, a core of "independistas" had agitated for independence for the island, which became a U.S. possession following the Spanish-American War. By and large, Puerto Ricans have been satisfied with the commonwealth status of their island—it is neither a state nor an independent country. Over the years, American political leaders have offered to let Puerto Ricans decide for themselves how they want their country governed. One of those political leaders was President Harry Truman. Despite Truman's commitment to Puerto Rican self-determination, the independistas targeted the president for assassination. On November 1, 1950, two radical independistas tried to break into Blair House in Washington, where Truman and his family were living while the White House was under renovation. Their attempt to assassinate the president failed when Secret Service agents and security guards thwarted the plan.

Still, the independistas resolved to take violent steps to win independence. On March 1, 1954, three Puerto Rican terrorists smuggled guns into the gallery that overlooks the House of Representatives in the U.S. Capitol and sprayed gunfire down on some 250 members of Congress. Several members were injured but, miraculously, no one was killed.

In the Fraunces Tavern case, police quickly rounded up the

1954 saw a bizarre assault on Congress by members of a Puerto Rican nationalist group called FALN. Seeking Puerto Rican independence, three FALN members smuggled guns into the House of Representatives and opened fire. Luckily, no members of Congress were killed, and the attackers (two men and one woman) were quickly arrested.

terrorists. In all, 15 independistas were arrested, convicted and sentenced to lengthy prison terms. In 1999, President Bill Clinton offered clemency to the FALN members if they would renounce the use of violence. All but one of the imprisoned men agreed, and they were released.

One independista, Oscar López Rivera, refused Clinton's offer. He remains in jail and is not due to be released until the year 2050—when he will turn 107.

"I have no regrets for what I've done in the Puerto Rican independence movement," said López Rivera. "Would I be willing to renounce the struggle for Puerto Rico's independence to get out of jail? I will never do that."

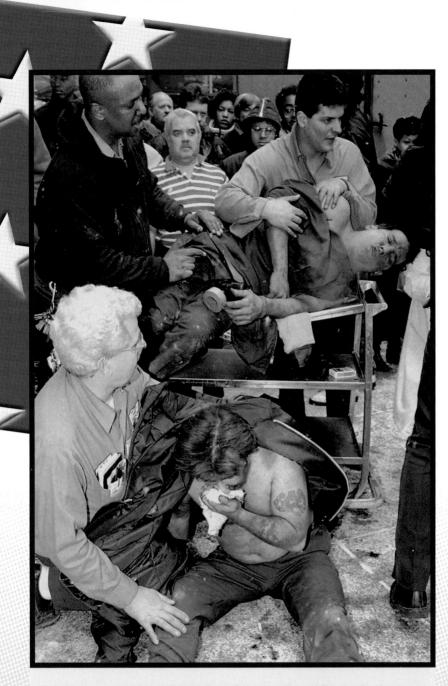

September 11th wasn't the first time the World Trade Center was attacked. In 1993 terrorists detonated a bomb in one of the basement parking garages, creating a smoky blast that killed 6 and injured 1,000. An investigation revealed an elaborate plot involving 22 conspirators, all of whom were eventually tracked down, tried, and imprisoned.

4

Modern-Day Terror

A lthough police quickly solved the Fraunces Tavern bombing, other terrorist groups resolved to target New York. By 1993, the cause of radical Islam had been brewing for years. Americans were first exposed to such terror in 1978, when fundamentalist Muslims in Iran led by exiled Ayatollah Ruhollah Khomeini over-threw the government of American-backed Shah Mohammad Reza Pahlavi. A year later, fanatical students taking their orders from Khomeini broke into the U.S. embassy in Tehran and took 63 diplomats hostage, holding them for more than a year until President Jimmy Carter could negotiate their release.

During the 1980s and early 1990s, many Muslims emigrated to America. Some of the more radical members of the Muslim community were drawn to a mosque in Jersey

City, New Jersey, where a cleric named Sheik Omar Abdel Rahman preached violence against the enemies of Islam.

"Hit hard and kill the enemies of God in every spot to rid the state of the descendants of the apes and pigs fed at the tables of Zionism, Communism and Imperialism," Rahman told his followers.

Rahman hatched a plan to wage a *jihad*, or holy war, against what he perceived to be the enemies of Islam. The cleric and his followers planned to blow up a series of monuments, bridges, tunnels, and buildings in New York City, including the Lincoln and Holland tunnels, United Nations Building, and FBI headquarters in Lower Manhattan. Their first target would be the World Trade Center.

Just after noon on February 26, 1993, a powerful bomb exploded in the basement parking garage of the World Trade Center, killing six people and injuring 1,000. Investigators would eventually conclude that the aim was to topple one of the twin towers into the other, sending both structures falling like titanic dominoes into lower Manhattan, killing as many as 250,000 people.

The towers did not fall, but in the buildings above the parking garage, chaos reigned. Lights flickered, then went dark. Elevators stuck between floors. Smoke rose from the basement to infiltrate the building's ventilation system. In the parking garage, the bomb opened up a 200-foot crater in the concrete. Damage to the building was estimated at $650 million.

At first, authorities weren't sure the explosion had been caused by a bomb. Could there have been a gas leak? New York Governor Mario Cuomo didn't need much convincing. "It looks like a bomb, it smells like a bomb—it's probably a bomb," Cuomo told reporters shortly after the blast. Cuomo suspected terrorists.

"No foreign people or force has ever done this to us," Cuomo said. "Until now, we were invulnerable."

Police soon confirmed Cuomo's suspicions. Sifting through the rubble in the parking garage, investigators came across a twisted piece of metal they identified as the chassis of a cargo van. Bomb experts inspected the chassis and concluded that it was at the center of the explosion. They estimated that the van held a 1,200-pound bomb made of the powerful explosive urea-nitrate.

Incredibly, investigators were able to find the van's vehicle identification number, or VIN, on the chassis. Once police had the VIN, it was a simple matter for them to trace the van to a truck rental agency in Jersey City. They learned the van had been rented three days before the World Trade Center bombing by a man named Mohammed Salameh. Police arrested the suspect when he returned to the rental agency to have his $200 deposit refunded, claiming the van had been stolen. In his pocket police found a copy of the rental contract he filled out to obtain the van. And on that rental contract was residue from the bomb-making chemicals.

Once Salameh was arrested, the other pieces started falling into place. One of the ringleaders was identified as Mahmud Abouhalima, who escaped to Egypt shortly after the bombing. Egyptian police arrested Abouhalima. He confessed and was extradited to the United States. From Abouhalima, police learned the names of 22 conspirators, including Sheik Omar Abdel Rahman. It took four years to track down all the conspirators, but all were eventually arrested, convicted and sentenced to lengthy prison terms.

By the late 1960s, New York had affirmed it place as not only America's largest city but also its center of trade and commerce. The city's Port Authority commissioned architect Minoru Yamasaki to design a structure that would emphasize New York's commercial power. After submitting several designs, the "twin towers" design was accepted, and in 1973 the World Trade Center was completed.

During the investigation, police first heard the name of an exiled Saudi Arabian millionaire who they believed provided the money to the conspirators to carry out the bombing.

The name of that man was Osama bin Laden.

Since September 11, 2001, the name Osama bin Laden has become infamous in the news. The son of a wealthy Saudi construction company owner, the terrorist leader used his personal fortune to fund the al-Qaeda network responsible for the World Trade Center attacks.

5

Retracing Al-Qaeda

Osama bin Laden emerged as a suspect in the September 11 bombing almost immediately. The son of a wealthy Saudi construction company owner, bin Laden had been introduced to radical Islamism while fighting against soldiers from the former Soviet Union who invaded Afghanistan in 1979. Thousands of rebels known as *mujahideen* fought a guerrilla war against the communist invaders, finally driving them out of the country in 1989. Many of the volunteers were Muslims from Middle East countries who flocked to Afghanistan to help the Islamic country fight off the Soviets. Bin Laden was one of those volunteers.

His experiences in Afghanistan hardened him to the role the United States played in that war. Through the Central Intelligence Agency, the U.S. had armed the mujahideen and provided other support, but when the Soviets pulled their army out of the country the Americans did nothing to establish a steady regime in Afghanistan. Soon, the country plunged into civil war.

Meanwhile, Iraqi forces under the command of dictator Saddam Hussein invaded neighboring Kuwait. The United States responded by leading an international coalition to drive the Iraqis off Kuwaiti land. The Persian Gulf War was largely staged from the deserts of Saudi Arabia. Bin Laden regarded the presence of western troops on Saudi soil a sacrilege.

Finally, bin Laden had long harbored a deep hatred for the Jewish state of Israel, which refused to give up territory so that Palestinians could establish a homeland. Since America was a steadfast supporter of Israel, bin Laden blamed the Americans for the plight of the Palestinians.

And so bin Laden used his personal fortune to establish an international terrorist group he named al-Qaeda, an Arabic word meaning "the base." Prior to September 11, 2001, al-Qaeda terrorists were believed to be responsible for at least two attacks on Americans. They included the simultaneous explosions of two bombs at U.S. embassies in Kenya and Tanzania, in which more than 270 people were killed, and the murders of 17 American sailors serving aboard the U.S. destroyer Cole, which was anchored in port in the Middle East nation of Yemen when a small boat pulled alongside of the vessel and suddenly exploded.

In addition, a routine check at a U.S.-Canada border crossing turned up a car laden with explosives; soon, authorities uncovered a plot to explode the bomb at Los Angeles International Airport. An investigation revealed al-Qaeda was behind that plan as well.

The Saudis had long since grown tired of bin Laden's support for terrorism and kicked him out of the country. He lived briefly in the North African nation of Sudan, but was expelled from there as well under pressure from American diplomats. Finally, he found a home in Afghanistan, where

As the grim task of recovering bodies from the World Trade Center attacks continued, law enforcement agencies at all levels began pursuing the case against al-Qaeda and bin Laden.

the fundamentalist Islamic regime known as the Taliban had taken power following the country's civil war. In Afghanistan, bin Laden set up terrorist training camps and began making plans for war on America and its allies.

As New Yorkers began the grim process of digging through the rubble for the bodies of the victims on September 11, 2001, law enforcement agencies not only in America but across the world began putting together the case against bin Laden and al-Qaeda.

In America, the investigation was headed by the FBI, although the bureau was assisted by a variety of other federal agencies, including the Central Intelligence Agency, National Security Agency, Federal Aviation Administration, National Transportation Safety Board as well as state and local police departments.

To begin with, the FBI learned that bin Laden had boasted weeks before the attack that he planned a terror strike on America. Indeed, he told the Arabic newspaper al-Quds that his terrorists would hit American targets.

"Personally, we received information that (bin Laden) planned very, very big attacks against American interests," said al-Quds editor Abdel-Bari Atwan. "We received several warnings like this. We did not take it so seriously."

Within hours, the National Security Agency, which specializes in gathering intelligence through spy satellites and other electronic methods, intercepted cellular phone transmissions from suspected bin Laden operatives in which they discussed the attacks.

Armed with that information, the FBI was able to identify the hijackers aboard the four planes. The agency made the identifications by obtaining the passenger lists from the airlines and tracking down the backgrounds of people on the lists. The FBI identified 18 people whose backgrounds linked them to radical Islamic activities.

The FBI pieced together the plan. Months before the attack, al-Qaeda had placed dozens of operatives in America with orders to enroll in commercial flight training schools.

The 18 men were split into four groups. They boarded two planes in Boston, one in Newark and one in Washington. They selected a Tuesday morning for the attack, which is normally a quiet time at American airports. They selected transcontinental flights because the planes' fuel tanks would be fully loaded. For weapons, they armed themselves with utility knives. While they are normally used to cut open cartons, the knives can still prove deadly. Clearly, the security measures at the airports where the terrorists boarded their flights were unable to detect the box cutters.

Once aboard the planes, the terrorists forced their way into the cockpits where they overpowered the crews. It is believed they killed crew members with the box cutters. Then, they took the controls and turned off the planes' transponders, which are beacons that alert air traffic controllers on the ground of the jets' locations in the air. Finally, they aimed for their targets.

Only the terrorists aboard United Airlines Flight 93 failed in their mission. The plane left Boston, then made a turn away from its planned route and headed for Washington. But the passengers aboard Flight 93 resolved to fight back and the plane crashed in the Pennsylvania countryside.

"This was well-funded and well-planned," said U.S. Senator Pat Roberts, a member of the Senate Intelligence Committee of the September 11 hijackings. "It took a lot of planning. The weather had to be just so on the East Coast. They used sophisticated tactics where they hijacked planes, killed the crew, and they had aviators or navigators who knew what they were doing."

The trail soon led the FBI to Huffman Aviation, a flight school in Venice, Florida, which is about 80 miles south of Tampa. FBI agents descended on the town, questioned the flight school's owners, seized their business records and showed photographs of the suspected terrorists to area residents.

Rudi Dekkers, owner of the school, identified two of the students as Mohammed Atta and Marwan al-Shehhi. Dekkers said the two men each paid $10,000 in cash for their tuition, and took lessons for five months before passing a commercial flight test administered by the Federal Aviation Administration. Dekkers said he hadn't seen the two men in nearly a year. As the investigation continued, it became clear to FBI agents that Atta

911

The number 911 was designated by AT&T in 1968 as the universal emergency number that people would call to report a crime, fire or accident. The first community in America to adopt the 911 emergency number was Haleyville, Alabama, and the first 911 call was placed in Haleyville on February 16, 1968. It was up to local police and fire departments and ambulance units to adopt the number, and it is now believed that 911 service is available to some 95% of the United States.

Following the trail of suspected terrorists, law enforcement officials quickly identified Mohamed Atta (seen here) and others, who used U.S. flight schools to train for their attacks on the World Trade Center and Pentagon.

was the leader of the mission to hijack the four planes.

In Vero Beach, Florida, a city up the coast from Miami, FBI agents determined that several of the terrorists attended the Flight Safety Academy and made their homes nearby. Several of the terrorists rented homes along 57th Terrace, a street in Vero Beach.

Elsewhere, the FBI found other leads. At Logan Airport in Boston, the agents learned that some of the hijackers had entered the United States through Canada by car, then took a flight from Portland, Maine, to Boston. Evidence that the terrorists received help from al-Qaeda members in New Jersey and Florida was also unearthed.

Within days of the bombings, dozens of suspects were taken into custody and held for questioning. Most of the suspects were citizens of Middle East countries whose visas had expired, meaning they were illegally in the country. Because of their illegal status, American law enforcement agencies had wide-ranging power to hold them that they wouldn't ordinarily be able to exercise against American citizens or legal aliens.

The data recorders in the jets that crashed into the Pentagon and the Pennsylvania countryside were recovered by investigators from the National Transportation Safety Board who

Because of the heroic acts of a few, not all the terrorist attacks of September 11th achieved their goals. Recent evidence suggests that when passengers aboard hijacked Flight 93 learned of their fate, they banded together to seize control of the plane, forcing it down in a field near Somerset, Pa. Although all aboard were killed in the crash, the quick action of the passengers and crew likely saved many more lives.

sifted through the debris of the planes. But in the two World Trade Center crashes, the data recorders were never found. They remained buried somewhere beneath the 1.25 million tons of concrete, steel and glass that came tumbling down on September 11. What the hijackers in the cockpits said to one another as their planes approached the World Trade Center may never be known.

"Of course, we know what happened on September 11 but it goes beyond that," said FBI spokesman Joseph Valiquette. "We don't know what was said in the cockpits, by the crew members or the hijackers. Is there language implicating other individuals who might have been involved? Is al-Qaeda mentioned? Is there idle chatter about other plans for that day or subsequently?"

In a showing of strength and solidarity, American troops in Afghanistan raise an American flag above the Kandahar airport. The flag, flown over Ground Zero in New York shortly after the terrorist attacks, was donated to the Marines by the NYPD and bears the names of many who died on September 11.

The Battle is Joined

J ust 26 days after the terrorist attacks on the World Trade Center and Pentagon, President George W. Bush ordered air strikes on Afghanistan. It took law enforcement agencies just a few days to gather enough evidence to convince the president that Osama bin Laden had masterminded the attacks. Bush demanded that the Taliban government turn over bin Laden and his top lieutenants to the United States; the Taliban refused. It didn't take long for the president's patience to wear thin.

And so, just after 9 P.M. on the night of October 7, 2001, American bombers aided by planes from Great Britain flew into Afghan air space and commenced a relentless bombing campaign against the Taliban and al-Qaeda.

"The battle is now joined on many fronts," Bush told Americans in a nationally televised address. "We will not waver. We will not tire. We will not falter. And we will not fail. Peace and freedom will prevail."

American and British troops soon arrived on the ground in Afghanistan. They were aided by Afghans who fought for the so-called Northern Alliance, a ragtag group of rebels who opposed the Taliban government. With the backing of American and British firepower, the tide of the civil war against the Taliban soon turned in favor of the rebels. Taliban and al-Qaeda forces were routed throughout the country. A new government friendly to America was installed in the Afghan capital of Kabul.

Bin Laden remained defiant. The elusive al-Qaeda leader fled to Afghanistan's mountains, where he directed al-Qaeda's military strategy from a cave. He also made videotaped messages and had them smuggled out of Afghanistan for broadcast on Al-Jazeera, a television station based in the Persian Gulf nation of Qatar.

"There is America, hit by God in one of its softest spots," bin Laden boasted on one tape. "Its greatest buildings were destroyed, thank God for that."

Throughout the bombing campaign, bin Laden had urged his followers to continue the attacks on America. To guard against further strikes by terrorists, governments in the United States took dramatic steps to guard the safety of Americans. Security at airports was made stricter. Security at government buildings was also tightened. Hundreds of other steps were taken.

To coordinate the nation's response to the threat of terrorism, President Bush selected Pennsylvania Governor Tom Ridge to head a new agency named the Office of Homeland Security. Soon, Ridge and Bush crafted a plan to spend some $38 billion to improve security. One of the first programs implemented by Ridge was the creation of a federal police force to provide security at airports. The

Osama bin Laden became a familiar face to the world as television stations showed videoclips from bin Laden's own taped messages, or scenes from his personal life, such as this excerpt from his son's wedding.

force of "sky marshals" would include 30,000 employees to screen baggage at the nation's busy airports.

Another proposal by Ridge was to devote about $10 billion to enhancing security at America's borders. That job is performed by the U.S. Immigration and Naturalization Service, but in recent years the INS has concerned itself mostly with apprehending illegal immigrants from Latin American countries who attempt to sneak into Texas, New Mexico, Arizona and California. Under Ridge's plan, the INS would be authorized to hire more agents to monitor the activities of aliens, and making sure that aliens with expired visas leave the country. In the September 11 attacks, many of the suspects were found to have remained in America after their visas expired.

Some of the money would go to local police departments to help them establish anti-terrorism programs. And, finally, Ridge proposed that $6 billion be spent on preventing bioterrorism—the use of deadly biological agents to spread disease and infections.

The need to combat bioterrorism became clear to government leaders soon after the September 11 attacks when several people on the East Coast contracted the rare disease anthrax. Found mostly in farm animals but also developed by countries as a weapon, the spores can be passed through contact with infected skin, but they can also be inhaled. Anthrax sufferers develop skin rashes, high fevers and other flu-like symptoms. The disease can be fatal, but antibiotics are effective and most anthrax sufferers who receive treatment are able to recover.

In early October 2001 employees of a tabloid newspaper publisher in Florida contracted the disease. Next, letters addressed to NBC news anchor Tom Brokaw and Senate Majority Leader Tom Daschle were found to have been contaminated with a powdery substance that contained anthrax spores. From their postmarks, FBI agents were able to determine the letters passed through a post office near Trenton, New Jersey. Some employees at the post office who handled the letters contracted the disease. The search for a suspect centered on the Trenton area, but despite months of investigation in which hundreds of people were interviewed, FBI agents were unable to identify a suspect. Certainly, law enforcement agencies believed al-Qaeda operatives remained in the United States following the September 11 attacks and there was no question that bin Laden's terrorists were among the list of suspects thought to have sent the letters to Daschle, Brokaw and others, but they were never able to turn up substantial proof that al-Qaeda was to blame. Eventually the FBI began to suspect a domestic source— possibly a U.S. scientist who had worked with man-made anthrax in U.S. Army laboratories.

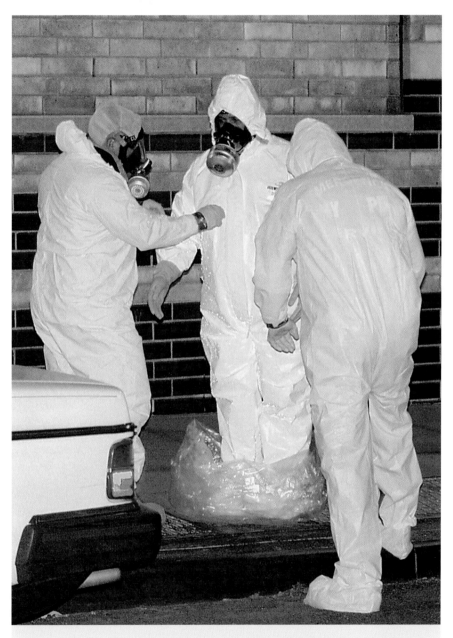

Following the September 11th terrorist attacks, a new threat emerged. Letters containing the deadly bacteria anthrax began arriving at the offices of government officials and the news media. Preparing for such acts of "bioterrorism" challenged law enforcement officials to draw up new plans to keep us safe from contaminated mail.

Twenty-three New York City police officers gave their lives trying to aid victims of the September 11 terrorist attacks. At a ceremony honoring those who made the ultimate sacrifice, Patricia Smith, the two-year-old daughter of officer Moira Smith wears the Medal of Honor posthumously awarded to her mother.

Law enforcement agencies were starting to feel the strain of the paranoia that the nation was feeling in the wake of September 11 and the anthrax attacks. Many reports of anthrax turned out to be false alarms; additionally, police across the country were stretching their manpower to the limit trying to tackle the threat of domestic terrorism while still performing their main duties of enforcing the law.

On December 5, 2001, the New York Police Department honored the officers killed in the September 11 World Trade Center attack. Each of the 23 police officers who died in the attack was awarded the Medal of Honor, the NYPD's highest award for valor. New York Mayor Rudolph Giuliani presented the medals, which were accepted by the family members of the dead police officers. The event was held in Carnegie Hall, the famed concert hall where some of the world's greatest musicians have performed.

NYPD Officer James Smith and his 2-year-old daughter Patricia accepted the award for Moira Smith. The policeman and little girl strode to the center of the stage, where Mayor Giuliani bent over and placed the medal, a gold star weighing eight pounds, around Patricia's neck.

After the ceremony, friends gathered around the Smiths. James Smith lifted the toddler into his arms and placed his uniform hat atop his daughter's head. Smith spent a few more minutes talking with well-wishers, then headed for an exit. Patricia's father carried her out of Carnegie Hall, into the vast city her mother had given her life to protect.

Canedy, Dana, and Sanger, David E. "The Suspects: Hijacking Trail Leads FBI to Florida Flight School." *The New York Times*, September 13, 2001.

Daly, Michael. "Little Girl as Special as Her NYPD Mom." *New York Daily News*, December 5, 2001.

Dunlap, David W. "Towers Lent City a Lift, Adding Postcard Panache and an Air of Resilience." *The New York Times*, September 13, 2001.

Filkins, Dexter. "Alive: Entombed for a Day, Then Found." *The New York Times*, September 13, 2001.

Fitzgerald, Jim. "Last World Trade Center Survivor Released From Hospital." The Associated Press, January 18, 2002.

Gibbs, Nancy. "If You Want to Humble an Empire." *Time*, Special September 11, 2001, edition.

Kapstatter, Bob. "Hundreds Dead Among Finest and the Bravest." *New York Daily News*, September 12, 2001.

Lardner, James, and Repetto, Thomas. *NYPD: A City and Its Police*. New York: Henry Holt and Company, 2000.

Landers, Jim. "Bin Laden Tape Appeals for War on U.S." *Dallas Morning News*, October 8, 2001.

Lathem, Niles. "Experts Sure It's Bin Laden's Work." *The New York Post*, September 12, 2001.

Lumpkin, John J. "U.S. Seeks DNA Samples from Bin Laden's Family." The Associated Press, February 28, 2002.

Marcovitz, Hal. *Terrorism*. Philadelphia: Chelsea House Publishers, 2000.

Miller, Adam. "A Scrapbook from Ground Zero." *Pet Life*, January-February 2002.

Pyle, Richard. "No Luck Finding Two Planes' Recorders."
The Associated Press, February 24, 2002.

Roosevelt, Theodore. *An Autobiography*. New York: Da Capo
Press, 1985.

Sack, Kevin, and Yardley, Jim. "U.S. Says Hijackers Lived in the Open
With Deadly Secret." *The New York Times*, September 14, 2001.

Sen, Indrani. "He Made His Colleagues Feel Safe." *Newsday*,
October 11, 2001.

Soltis, Andy. "Bin Laden's Sick Boast Now Realty."
The New York Post, September 12, 2001.

Thomma, Steven. "Bush Launches 'Relentless' Campaign;
Defiant Bin Laden Makes New Threat." *The Philadelphia
Inquirer*, October 8, 2001.

Weiss, Lois. "5 Years to Build, 90 Minutes to Destroy."
The New York Post, September 12, 2001.

Wright, Lawrence. "The Counter-Terrorist." *The New Yorker*,
January 14, 2002.

"Wall Street Explosion Kills 30, Injures 300; Morgan Office Hit,
Bomb Pieces Found." *The New York Times*, September 17, 1920.

http://www.911dispatch.com/911_file/history/911history.html
  [History of 911]

http://www.torontopolice.on.ca/pds/histdog1.html
  [The History of Dogs in Police Work]

http://community-2.webtv.net/Hahn-50thAP-K9/K9History30/
  [Police Dog History]

http://www.nycpolicemuseum.org
  [New York City Police Museum]

http://www.portauthoritypolicememorial.org
  [Port Authority Police Memorial]

Federal Aviation Administration
800 Independence Avenue, S.W.
Washington, DC 20591
www.faa.gov

Federal Bureau of Investigation
935 Pennsylvania Avenue, NW, Room 7972
Washington, DC 20535
www.fbi.gov

National Security Agency
www.nsa.gov

New York Police Department
http://www.nyc.gov/html/nypd/home.html

Port Authority of New York and New Jersey
http://www.panynj.gov

U.S. Immigration and Naturalization Service
http://www.ins.gov/graphics/index.htm

Lardner, James, and Repetto, Thomas. *NYPD: A City and Its Police*. New York: Henry Holt and Company, 2000.

Marcovitz, Hal. *Terrorism*. Philadelphia: Chelsea House Publishers, 2000.

Nash, Jay Robert. *Terrorism in the 20th Century*. New York: M. Evans and Co., 1998.

Roosevelt, Theodore. *An Autobiography*. New York: Da Capo Press, 1985.

Afghanistan
  bin Laden in, 44-45
  bombing campaign against, 51-52
  Soviet invasion of, 43-44
Airports, security at, 52-53
Al-Qaeda, 44, 45-49, 51-52, 54
Al-Shehhi, Marwan, 47
Anarchist movement, 27-31
Anthrax, 54, 57
Atta, Mohammed, 47-48

Bennett, James Gordon, 18-20
Bin Laden, Osama, 41, 43-49, 51, 52, 54
Bioterrorism, preventing, 54, 57
Borders, security at, 53
Bush, George W., 51-52
Byrnes, Thomas, 23, 24

Congress, and Puerto Rican terrorists, 34
Constables, 18, 20
Federal Bureau of Investigation (FBI)
  and Palmer Raids, 28-29
  and September 11 attacks, 45-49

Flight schools, 47-48
Fraunces Tavern bombing, 32-35
Fuerzas Armadas de Liberacion Nacional
  (FALN), 32-35

Giuliani, Rudolph, 15, 57

Immigration and Naturalization Service, 53
Iran hostage crisis, 37

Jewett, Helen, 18-19

Lexow Committee, 23

McKinley, William, 28
McVeigh, Timothy, 32
Marshals, 18, 20
Murray, William, 23
Muslims, 37-38
  and Iran hostage crisis, 37
  and World Trade Center bombing, 10,
    37-39, 41
  See also September 11 terrorist attacks

New York Herald, 18-20

New York Police Department
  and Civil War draft riots, 20-22
  corruption in, 23-24
  creation of, 17-20
  and Fraunces Tavern bombing, 32-35
  and Irish police, 20
  reform of, 23-25
  and Wall Street bombing, 29-31
  and World Trade Center 9/11 attacks,
    9-15, 57
  and World Trade Center 1993 bombing,
    10, 37-39, 41
New York Sun, 18
Night watchmen, 18, 20
Northern Alliance, 52

Office of Homeland Protection, 52-54
Oklahoma City bombing, 32

Palmer Raids, 28-29
Penny press papers, 18-19
Puerto Rican terrorists, 32-35

Rahman, Omar Abdel, 38, 39
Ridge, Tom, 52-54
Roosevelt, Theodore, 23-25

September 11 terrorist attacks
  America's response to, 51-54, 57
  investigation of, 43-49
  and World Trade Center, 9-15, 49, 57

Taliban, 45, 51-52
Terrorism, 31-32
  and anarchism, 27-31
  and anthrax, 54, 57
  and Cole explosion, 44
  and embassy bombings, 44
  Iran hostage crisis, 37
  and Oklahoma City bombing, 32
  and Puerto Ricans, 32-35
  and World Trade Center 1993 bombing,
    10, 37-39, 41
  See also September 11 terrorist attacks
Truman, Harry, 34

Wall Street bombing, 29-31
World Trade Center
  and 1993 bombing, 10, 37-39, 41
  and September 11 attacks, 9-15, 49, 57

HAL MARCOVITZ is a journalist for *The Morning Call*, a newspaper based in Allentown, Pennsylvania. He has written more than 30 books for young readers, including books on terrorism, the war in the Balkans and the history of Jordan. He lives in Chalfont, Pennsylvania, with his wife, Gail, and daughters Ashley and Michelle.